MW01485023

A Gift For:

From:

Published by Hallmark Gift Books,
a division of Hallmark Cards, Inc.,
Kansas City, MO 64141
Visit us on the Web at Hallmark.com.

Editorial Director: Delia Berrigan
Art Director: Chris Opheim
Designer: Scott Swanson
Production Designer: Dan Horton
Writers: Bill Gray, Dan Taylor, Katherine Stano,
Ellen Brenneman, Meg Burik, Melissa Woo,
Cat Hollyer, Keely Chace

ISBN: 978-1-63059-649-1
BOK1437

Made in China
0519

Table of Contents

On Aging
and Exercise

I run my mouth, I lift my finger,
I jump from crabby to pissed...
with all this work, you'd think I'd be
in better shape than this!

I feel like I've been on the rack. I hit the gym and it hit back.

My back tattoo was really nice.
It had a lot of class.
Too bad that as the years went by
it drifted to my ass.

With a few small improvements an exercise bike
could go from a "giant thumbs down" to a like.
If the seat were wider and a back part was added
and the whole thing was right by my TV, and padded.
I'd ride that bike, not a thing could be finer
if when you said bike, what you meant was recliner.

13

Folks at my gym
run fast every day.
I put on shorts.
They run away.

Graying. Wrinkles. Mystery spots.
Bags beneath the eyes.
Arteries stuffed full of muck.
Sag around the thighs.
Jiggly parts. Impromptu farts.
Puttin' on the weight.
Turning 29 again
sure is pretty great.

I have a beautician.
I've used her for years.
She's quite the magician
with curlers and shears.
There's a reason why
I'm so loyal, it's true:
she mixes the dye
my exact shade of blue.

I used to tweeze hairs
that were gray.
But then, more appeared
the next day.
So I guess with gray hairs
I am stuck.
Which leads me to say,
"What the pluck?"

I wheeze
when I sneeze.
There's pain in my knees.
I'm stooped,
I'm pooped,
my boobs have drooped.
I'm graying,
decaying,
time passes. Just saying.
Got a gut,
but so what?
I can still kick some butt.

I work out every single day,
sometimes more than once.
I do all kinds of stretches
and lots of flexing stunts.
You'd be amazed to witness it,
I work out like a champ.
There's just no way I'm gonna risk
a middle finger cramp.

People my age still have sex,
that's absolutely true!
We love to let our hair down,
even if that hair is blue.
People my age still have sex,
we really let it rip!
It's only every now and then
that someone breaks a hip.

Food
and Booze

Here's some stuff I'm thankful for:
nacho chips and dip galore.
Don't have to diet anymore.
When relatives go out the door.
Dogs to lick food off the floor.
Folks who cower when I roar.
I'm wiser than in days of yore.
A pillow for a butt that's sore.
Every housecoat that I wore.
All the f**kin' times I swore.
Beer. How 'bout we have some more?

Tonight, I have an awesome date.
Surprisingly, I just can't wait.
He's sweet and smooth and like a dream.
The flavor-of-the-month ice cream!

I really like to sip on tea.
It always helps me to unwind.
Especially when that pitcher's filled
with the chilled Long Island kind!

I love a buffet
where the veggies are cooked
until they're a mush
of broccoligook.
Where the chicken is greasy
and the gravy has skin
and there's nothing to eat
if you plan to stay thin.
Where the rib's not quite prime,
the steak's mostly gristle,
and the waitress gets testy
whenever you whistle.

Where the cheap paper napkins
slide off your lap
and there's some sort of pie.
Cherry, perhaps?
The plates all have chips,
the tables are dusty,
the green beans are brown,
and the taters are crusty.
The milk has an odor,
the tea is too sweet.
So, why do I love it?
It's all-you-can-eat!

Why is the food that's so bad for you
so good? C'mon! You know it's true!
Cookies and donuts and chocolaty treats
taste so much better than broccoli and beets.
Celery sticks? They don't have what it takes.
And carrots? OK, if they're part of a cake.
So here's my advice if you ask me to dinner:
salad's a loser, dessert is a winner.
But if we sit down to a big bowl of veggies,
you best be prepared for some noogies or wedgies.

The stuff in the back of my fridge, truth be told,
has been there a while and is painted with mold.
Which leaves me here puzzling this mystery:
what in the heck did this glop used to be?

Holidays and Relatives

'Twas the month of December,
and all through my house,
relatives gathered,
including each spouse.
I grimaced and griped,
almost pulled out my hair,
in hopes they would see
I did not want them there.
And I, with my attitude
('cause of their crap),
just wanted to go
take a long winter's nap.
I finally shouted
and called them by name,

"Out cousins! Out brats!
Have you not any shame?
Make your way to the door!
Look, it's right down the hall!
Now, take a hike! Take a hike!
Take a hike, all!"
Once we were done
with our annual fight,
I watched as they finally
drove out of sight.
My eyes, how they twinkled!
I felt all aglow!
Merry Crabmas, my fam!
You had me at..."Let's go."

If you want me there
for your big wedding day,
don't have it in Maui
and expect me to pay.

40

Jingle bells, something smells, think I burnt the roast. Sorry, everybody, but instead, we're having toast.

Away in a caftan,
with room for my butt.
You won't see my droopage.
Not stylish? So what?
The stars in the sky
don't care what I wear.
I love my big caftan,
it's comfy, so THERE.

Up on the countertop, sponges pause—
my cleanliness has major flaws.
Sure, I could clean up, but cleaning stinks.
Maybe instead, I'll fix a drink.

Jolly old brassiere of mine,
lean your cups this way.
Hold 'em steady, hold 'em high—
never let 'em sway!

Changing Seasons

Spring is the reason
I'm wheezin' and sneezin',
which I don't find pleasin'.
Plus, there are bees 'n'
mosquitoes 'n' fleas 'n'
I just hate this season!

I thought it'd be fun
to get out in the sun.
Now I'm red as a lobster,
and mean as a mobster,
with a face that is feelin'
like it's gonna start peelin'.
Did you notice how "summer"
rhymes so well with "bummer"?

Came home from the beach
with a question in mind:
How'd I get sand
where the sun doesn't shine?

The driveway's slick
as polished glass.
Ol' Man Winter's
a pain in the ass.

It's fun at the pool.
I'm sure you'd agree.
But you're probably soaking
in preschooler pee.

I planned to fertilize my lawn.
Spring's the time you need to do it.
But then I saw the dog next door
had gone and beat me to it.

AN ODE TO SUMMER

The clouds are puffy in the sky
as butterflies go flitting by.
The breezes make the flowers dance
and I have sweaty underpants.

If the temperatures are falling,
here's a way to make it better:
when the frost is on your pumpkins,
grab the nearest ugly sweater.

I'm getting sick of shoveling,
high heat bills, and the rest.
Hey Floyd, let's hitch the sled up—
and aim it toward Key West!

The beach is hot
and I am not,
so look the other way.
I'm not here for a fashion shoot.
You've been warned, OK?

All this winter snow can scram
'cause I'm fresh outta give-a-damn!
I'm hunkered down in my cocoon
and never coming out 'til June!

Dealing with ants is no picnic.
This summer, they've been really bad!
If this sh*t continues, I'll do something drastic
and clean up my kitchen a tad!

It's finally nice and warm enough to bust out the ol' flip-flops... but enough about what's going on inside my saggy swimsuit top!

When a chill is in the autumn air
and windshields have to thaw,
when the frost is on the pumpkins,
guess I need a warmer bra.

The pollen
that's fallen
is the reason
I'm sneezing.

In the air there's a feeling
of snot that's congealing
on mustaches, beards, and goatees.
It's crusty and stanky.
Please! Use a hanky!
Stop ruining Christmas for me!

Work Life

I love to work!
It's lots of fun,
especially seeing everyone!
My frenemies.
The boss's pet.
That dude who snores.
The dumb bimbette.
Those morning people
full of sh*t.
The interns

I must babysit.
The slacker
I'd be pleased to punch.
The criminal
who steals my lunch.
The idiots
who make my day...
as long as they just
STAY AWAY!

I wave bye-bye
and say "See ya later!!"
right after I fart
in the elevator.

My office is really a beehive.
The evidence seems pretty clear.
Every time managers open their traps,
buzzwords are all that I hear.

Company picnics are just not my thing.
I don't like to network or schmooze.
Here's a fun tip: just stay out of my way.
I'm only there for the booze.

There's a reason my desk
is littered with papers
and much miscellaneous crap.
I mush them together
and make a big pile,
for a pillow when I take a nap.

People,
Am I Right?

Roses are red.
Violets are blue.
I don't like most people.
But I tolerate you!

You see the good in everyone.
Your sweetness is unending.
You're just the kind of person
that I'm sure I won't be friending.

Make new friends
but keep the old.
In case all the new ones
turn into A-holes.

Your cat.

Your dog.

The furniture that sits out in your lawn.

A salad.

And a cozy quilt.

Something a kid has drawn.

I've looked at all the photos

that you've got stored on your phone.

I "oohed" and "ahhed" and nicely nod,

now please leave me alone.

I think I'd like a Tiny House.
They're cute in their own way.
And, when a neighbor's buggin' me,
I'd simply drive away!

Social Media and Entertainment

A Pinterest page
for folks my age
is mostly shots
of liver spots.

Don't "Like" my posts?
Our friendship is toast.

People who renovate homes on TV
have us all hooked. That's easy to see.
Tearing out kitchens, plastering walls,
tuckpointing chimneys, and repainting halls.
Breaking a sweat as they work really fast,
while I sip a cold one and sit on my ass.

Every now and then
I might consider swiping right.
But then remember I prefer
to sleep alone at night!

If in the real world we meet,
don't ask me if I "liked" your tweet.
Did I see your post? I doubt it.
Why would I wanna talk about it?
Having an online conversation
only gives me consternation.

Fashion

No lingerie, designer pants—
who needs that fancy stuff?
When I'm in bed I sleep just fine
alone and in the buff!

Trying to look sexy
at my age is tough.
My blouse is lo-cut,
but not near low enough.

My swimsuit's really out of date.
Why the hell should I hide it?
If "old and saggy" really bugs you,
don't look at what's inside it!

New rule: If we could wear it
when we were young and hot,
we can't when it comes back in style,
especially now that we're not!

200 bucks for holey jeans?
I've got that look for free!
My ratty "vintage" denim
is as "boho" as can be!

Strappy little summer tops.
Cutoffs up to here.
Belly shirts, G-strings, and teeny thongs?
Well, never fear.
I won't wear this crap
any time of year.
(You're welcome.)

Nothing like a beach chair,
a book, a spot of shade,
a drink or three,
some snacks, some tunes,
and Speedos on parade!

Not saying I'd bring back the days when men wore suits and ties— but enough with all the cargo shorts! My eyes! My eyes! My eyes!

Elastic waists,
one-size-fits-all,
bras with unicups—
and athleisure's just a fancy way
of saying "I give up!"

General
Crabby
Philosophy
and Politics

You don't know mean
'til you've met the queen.
Being crabby's my biz.
That's right. I'm Maxine.

While stuck here in traffic
I know what's the matter:
extra-large coffee
and extra-small bladder.

Hey, morning people?
Stay out of my sight.
Say "Have a nice day!"
And you're in for a fight.

I have a middle finger.
It's sturdy, and I praise it.
It's always right there, handy.
Nothing seems to faze it.
And if you piss me off today,
you'll likely see me raise it.

If the rooster crows
at the break of dawn,
it'll shortly discover
that its head is now gone.

Where do socks go when they're suddenly gone?
Are they up in sock heaven? The great sock beyond?
Another dimension? A sock Twilight Zone?
Leaving their mates as they move on alone?
I can't help thinking they're out there somewhere,
laughing at me holding half of a pair.

I think politicians are really magicians.
If you're into tricks they sure got 'em.
Year after year, they make cash disappear
down a rathole without any bottom.

Politicians say a lot
and spend a ton to boot.
To "thank" them for their service...
I'll give 'em THIS salute!

124

You don't have to ask me twice.
I'm always ready with advice.
A tip, a hint, a nudge, a trick.
I've got the answer super-quick!
Check with me? Here's why you might:
I'm always absolutely right!

I wrote things on a sticky note
but don't know where I stuck it.
When that happens, I just say—
"Well, you know what? ...Don't worry about it."

Maxine is all done
using verses to whine.
Let us know what you thought!
Please drop us a line.

Please write a review at Hallmark.com,
e-mail us at booknotes@hallmark.com,
or send your comments to:

Hallmark Book Feedback
P.O. Box 419034
Mail Drop 100
Kansas City, MO 64141